NORTHUMBERLAND

TRAVEL GUIDE 2025

Explore Castles, Coastlines, and Countryside in England's Hidden Gem

Kenneth Marlow

© 2025 BY KENNETH MARLOW
ALL RIGHTS RESERVED

No part of this publication may be reproduced, stored in a retrieval system, or transmitted in any form or by any means, electronic, mechanical, photocopying, recording, or otherwise, without the prior written permission of the copyright owner.

DISCLAIMER

This book is for informational purposes only. While every effort has been made to ensure accuracy, the author and publisher make no warranties and assume no responsibility for errors, omissions, or any outcomes resulting from its use. Travel conditions, prices, and regulations may change; readers are encouraged to verify details independently. The author and publisher are not liable for any decisions or actions taken based on this book.

Northumberland Travel Guide 2025

TABLE OF CONTENTS

Introduction.. 8
  Welcome to Northumberland: England's Best-Kept Secret... 8
  Why Visit Northumberland in 2025?................ 9
  A Brief History of Northumberland................. 11
  How to Use This Guide....................................... 12
Chapter 1: Planning Your Trip..................... 14
  Best Time to Visit Northumberland................. 14
  How to Get to Northumberland (By Car, Train, Air)... 15
  Getting Around: Public Transport, Car Rentals, and Walking Routes.. 16
  Travel Tips & Essential Information................ 17
Chapter 2: Top Attractions in Northumberland... 19
  Hadrian's Wall & Roman Heritage................... 19
  Magnificent Castles & Historic Sites............... 24
  Northumberland's Natural Wonders............... 29
  Charming Towns & Villages............................ 34
Chapter 3: The Northumberland Coast – Beaches, Trails & Wildlife.......................... 41
  The Northumberland Coast Path: A Walk Through History and Nature........................... 41
  Bamburgh Beach: Golden Sands Beneath a Mighty Castle... 43
  Embleton Bay: A Photographer's Dream........ 45

Druridge Bay: A Hidden Coastal Gem............ 47
Coquet Island: Puffins, Seals, and a Lighthouse. 49

Chapter 5: Romantic Getaways – Best Places for Couples... 51

Luxury Retreats with Stunning Views............ 52
Most Romantic Castles & Historic Spots......... 55
Secluded Beaches for Couples......................... 58
Best Restaurants for a Romantic Dinner........ 61
The Treehouse Restaurant at Alnwick Gardens. 62

Chapter 6: Senior-Friendly Travel in Northumberland... 65

Easiest Walks with Stunning Views................ 65
Coastal Paths with Benches and Rest Stops.... 67
Historic Sites with Easy Access....................... 69
Alnwick Castle & Gardens (Mobility-Friendly).. 69
Cragside House: Beautiful Landscapes Without Strenuous Hiking... 70
Relaxing Activities for Seniors......................... 72
Scenic Train Rides Through Northumberland 74
Best Accommodations for Comfort & Accessibility... 75
Cozy Cottages with Easy Walking Distance to Attractions... 77

Chapter 7: Food & Drink in Northumberland... 79

Traditional Northumbrian Dishes You Must
Try.. 79
The Best Seafood Restaurants & Pubs............. 81
Where to Try Lindisfarne Mead...................... 82
Northumberland's Best Tea Rooms & Cafés... 82

Chapter 8: Where to Stay – Accommodation for Every Traveler... 84

Luxury Stays: Castle Hotels & Boutique Inns. 84
Budget-Friendly Guesthouses & Hostels......... 88
Cozy Cottages & Self-Catering Retreats.......... 92
Unique Stays: Glamping, Yurts & Farmstays.93

Chapter 9: Family-Friendly Northumberland... 95

Best Attractions for Kids.................................. 95
Wildlife Parks & Farm Experiences............... 100
Interactive Castle Experiences for Families.. 101

Chapter 10: Hidden Gems & Off-the-Beaten-Path Adventures.............. 104

The Secret Waterfalls of Northumberland.... 104
Remote Villages with Stunning Views........... 107
The Mysterious Duddo Stone Circle............... 110
Lesser-Known Ruins & Historic Sites............. 111

Chapter 11: Events & Festivals in Northumberland 2025............................... 113

Alnwick International Music Festival............ 113
The Berwick Film & Media Arts Festival........ 115
Northumberland County Show..................... 116

Kielder Winter Wonderland............................117
Chapter 12: Practical Travel Tips & Final Thoughts.. 119
   Packing List for Northumberland.................. 119
   Safety Tips for Exploring Remote Areas....... 120
   Best Apps and Websites for Travel Planning. 121
   Responsible Tourism: Protecting Northumberland's Natural Beauty................122
Bonus Chapter... 124
MAPS..132

Northumberland Travel Guide 2025

INTRODUCTION

Welcome to Northumberland: England's Best-Kept Secret

If you've never heard of Northumberland, don't worry—you're not alone. Nestled in the northeast of England, it's one of the country's most overlooked gems. And honestly? That's part of its charm. While tourists swarm to London, York, or the Lake District, Northumberland remains wild, unspoiled, and gloriously empty in all the best ways.

But don't mistake its tranquility for dullness. This is a land of mighty castles perched on dramatic cliffs, Roman ruins whispering tales of ancient conquests, and rugged coastlines that seem to stretch into eternity. It's a place where you can hike all morning and not see another soul, then find yourself in a centuries-old pub by evening, warming up with a pint by a roaring fire.

Whether you're a history buff, a nature lover, or simply someone looking for a break from the ordinary, Northumberland has something for you. And by the time you finish this book, I have a feeling you'll wonder why you hadn't visited sooner.

Why Visit Northumberland in 2025?

So why should you pack your bags for Northumberland *this* year? Well, for starters, it's a place where time seems to have hit the pause button—but in the best possible way. Unlike the overcrowded tourist hotspots, Northumberland lets you breathe. No shuffling through crowds or queuing for hours just to get a glimpse of a landmark. Here, history and nature exist in their purest form, waiting for you to explore at your own pace.

But Northumberland isn't just about peace and quiet. In 2025, it's buzzing with new energy. Restoration projects have breathed new life into historic sites, new walking trails are opening up more of the stunning landscape, and local food scenes are having a moment (yes, I'm talking about more than just fish and chips). Whether you want to visit iconic castles like Bamburgh and Alnwick or discover the Dark Sky Park, where the stars look brighter than anywhere else in England, Northumberland in 2025 is a dream for adventurers and relaxation-seekers alike.

And let's not forget the wildlife—seals, puffins, and if you're lucky, dolphins playing off the coast. It's like stepping into a BBC nature documentary, only without David Attenborough narrating (unfortunately).

A Brief History of Northumberland

Northumberland's history isn't just long—it's **epic**. This land has seen everything: Roman legions marching along Hadrian's Wall, Viking raids striking fear into coastal villages, and medieval battles that shaped the very fate of England. If history had a greatest hits album, Northumberland would have several tracks on it.

Hadrian's Wall, built by the Romans in AD 122 to keep out the wild Scots, still stands today—though the Scots eventually made their way south anyway (and we're glad they did, because they brought whisky). Later, the region became a battleground between England and Scotland, with castles popping up faster than you can say "border conflict." These castles—Bamburgh, Alnwick, Warkworth, and more—are still standing, and wandering through them feels like stepping straight into a medieval movie set.

Northumberland also played a key role in early Christianity. The Holy Island of Lindisfarne was home to one of England's first monasteries, and its monks created the world-famous Lindisfarne Gospels, a stunning work of art that somehow survived Viking invasions and centuries of history.

And here's the best part: Northumberland hasn't been turned into a museum. Its history isn't behind glass—it's under your feet, in the air, and in the stones of its ancient ruins.

How to Use This Guide

This book isn't just about giving you a list of places to see. It's about helping you experience Northumberland like a true explorer. You'll find:

- **Detailed itineraries** to suit every kind of traveler, from history buffs to outdoor adventurers.
- **Hidden gems**—places most guidebooks overlook but are absolute must-visits.
- **Insider tips** on where to eat, stay, and avoid tourist traps.

- **Stories and legends** that bring the region's history to life (because let's be honest, history is a lot more fun with a few dramatic tales thrown in).
- **Practical advice** on getting around, the best times to visit, and how to make the most of your trip.

Think of this book as your personal travel companion—the kind that knows all the best spots, has a great sense of humor, and won't get mad if you ignore their advice and take a spontaneous detour (which, by the way, you absolutely should).

So, are you ready to uncover England's best-kept secret? Let's dive in. Northumberland is waiting.

CHAPTER 1: PLANNING YOUR TRIP

Best Time to Visit Northumberland

Northumberland is a destination that changes its character with the seasons, each offering a unique experience. The best time to visit largely depends on what you want to see and do.

- **Spring (March to May):** Expect blooming wildflowers, baby lambs in the fields, and pleasant walking weather. It's an excellent time for nature lovers and photographers.
- **Summer (June to August):** The busiest season, but with long daylight hours perfect for exploring castles, coastal paths, and Hadrian's

Wall. The Northumberland Coast shines during this time.
- **Autumn (September to November):** A golden-hued wonderland with fewer tourists, making it ideal for a peaceful getaway. The crisp air and stunning fall foliage make hiking an absolute pleasure.
- **Winter (December to February):** If you love dramatic landscapes, winter brings windswept beaches, cozy pubs, and a high chance of seeing the Northern Lights in the Northumberland Dark Sky Park.

No matter when you visit, Northumberland has a way of making every season feel like the perfect one.

How to Get to Northumberland (By Car, Train, Air)

Getting to Northumberland is relatively easy, but how you arrive will depend on your preferred mode of travel and starting location.

- **By Car:** If freedom and flexibility are priorities, driving is your best option. The **A1** is the main artery that connects Northumberland with London to the south and Edinburgh to the north.
- **By Train:** High-speed rail services from **London Kings Cross to Newcastle** take around **three hours**, with further connections

to **Alnmouth, Berwick-upon-Tweed, and Morpeth**.
- **By Air:** The closest major airport is **Newcastle International Airport**, offering domestic and international flights. From here, you can take a train or rent a car to explore the county.

Getting Around: Public Transport, Car Rentals, and Walking Routes

Northumberland is best explored at a leisurely pace, whether by car, public transport, or on foot.

- **Public Transport:** Buses link major towns and some villages, but schedules can be sparse in rural areas. Plan ahead!
- **Car Rentals:** The most convenient way to explore Northumberland's vast landscapes, remote castles, and scenic coastline. Be prepared for narrow country lanes and occasional sheep traffic jams.
- **Walking Routes:** Northumberland is a paradise for hikers, with trails like **Hadrian's Wall Path** and the **Northumberland Coast Path** offering breathtaking scenery and historical intrigue.

Travel Tips & Essential Information

Before you set off, here are some key travel tips to make your trip as smooth as possible:

- **Currency:** British Pound (£)
- **Language:** English (with charming Northumbrian and Geordie accents)
- **Weather:** Unpredictable. Always pack a raincoat and dress in layers.
- **Safety:** Northumberland is one of the safest places in the UK. Just watch out for unexpected waves on coastal paths and overenthusiastic seagulls eyeing your fish and chips.

- **Local Etiquette:** A friendly nod or "hello" goes a long way in smaller villages.

With your travel plans in place, you're ready to embark on an unforgettable journey through one of England's most remarkable regions. Now, let's dive into the must-see attractions that will make your trip truly special.

CHAPTER 2: TOP ATTRACTIONS IN NORTHUMBERLAND

Hadrian's Wall & Roman Heritage

Few places in England capture the imagination quite like **Hadrian's Wall**. Built in AD 122 under the orders of the Roman Emperor Hadrian, this **73-mile-long** fortification stretched across the northern frontier of the Roman Empire. Today, it stands as a UNESCO World Heritage Site, offering visitors a glimpse into the past through its well-preserved forts, milecastles, and museums.

Walking along the rugged remains of the Wall, you can almost hear the echoes of Roman soldiers who once patrolled this ancient boundary, keeping watch over the wild lands beyond. Let's dive into some of the most fascinating sites along this legendary structure.

Housesteads Roman Fort

Perched high on the windswept Whin Sill escarpment, **Housesteads Roman Fort** is one of the best-preserved Roman forts in Britain. Standing here, looking out over the rolling Northumberland landscape, you can easily picture life as a Roman soldier stationed on the empire's edge.

The fort's ruins include **barrack blocks, a hospital, granaries, and even one of Britain's oldest known toilets**—yes, a two-thousand-year-old latrine! The on-site museum provides fascinating artifacts, including weapons, pottery, and personal belongings left behind by the Roman occupants.

For an unforgettable experience, take a stroll along **Hadrian's Wall Path** from Housesteads—it's one of the most scenic sections of the wall, offering panoramic views that stretch for miles.

Vindolanda: A Glimpse into Roman Life

If Housesteads offer structure, **Vindolanda** provides soul. This extraordinary Roman fort and settlement is a working archaeological site, meaning new discoveries are constantly being unearthed.

Vindolanda is famous for the **Vindolanda Tablets**, a collection of handwritten wooden documents that reveal intimate details of daily life on the frontier. These letters and notes, preserved in the damp Northumbrian soil, include everything from birthday party invitations to complaints about army boots. One letter, written by a Roman woman to her sister, is considered one of the earliest examples of female handwriting in Britain.

Visitors can watch archaeologists at work, explore the reconstructed timber and stone forts, and wander through the immersive museum filled with treasures like leather shoes, jewelry, and Roman board games.

Pro tip: Visit between April and September for the chance to see live digs in action—there's nothing like witnessing history being uncovered before your eyes.

Chesters Roman Fort & Museum

Nestled beside the scenic River North Tyne, **Chesters Roman Fort** is the best-preserved cavalry fort along Hadrian's Wall. Built to house around **500 cavalrymen**, the fort still features remarkable remnants of bathhouses, barracks, and headquarters.

One of the highlights is the well-preserved **Roman baths**, where you can trace the layout of hot and cold rooms and imagine soldiers unwinding after a long day of patrolling the frontier. The adjacent **Chesters Museum** houses a fantastic collection of Roman altars, sculptures, and inscriptions—many of which were found right at the site.

If you fancy a leisurely stroll, the fort's riverside setting makes it one of the most picturesque spots along Hadrian's Wall. Pack a picnic and enjoy the view—just watch out for the local sheep who might try to share your lunch!

Hadrian's Wall isn't just a pile of ancient stones—it's a living testament to Northumberland's role in Roman Britain. Whether you're a history buff or simply love a good landscape, these sites offer a time-traveling experience like no other. And don't forget—this is just the beginning. There's plenty more to uncover in Northumberland's rich tapestry of history and culture!

Magnificent Castles & Historic Sites

Northumberland is a county where **castles aren't just relics—they're landmarks of power, legends, and untamed beauty**. From towering fortresses perched on coastal cliffs to romantic ruins whispering tales of the past, these castles are an absolute must-visit.

Bamburgh Castle: The King of Castles

Majestic. Dominating. Absolutely breathtaking. **Bamburgh Castle** is the crown jewel of Northumberland's coastline. Sitting proudly atop a volcanic outcrop, this mighty fortress has **over 1,400**

years of history and offers one of the most dramatic castle views in Britain.

Once the seat of the Anglo-Saxon kings, Bamburgh was later transformed into a formidable medieval stronghold. Walking through its grand halls, you'll find **ancient weaponry, suits of armor, and even tales of ghostly apparitions** said to roam the corridors at night.

The views from the castle walls? Simply jaw-dropping. Gaze out over the windswept beaches, where golden sands meet the North Sea, and if you're lucky, catch a glimpse of the Farne Islands in the distance.

Pro tip: Visit at sunset for a truly magical experience—the golden light makes the castle look like something straight out of a fantasy novel.

Alnwick Castle: A Magical Journey (Harry Potter Filming Location)

If Bamburgh is the King of Castles, then **Alnwick Castle** is the realm of enchantment. This **11th-century fortress** is one of the largest inhabited castles in England and has been home to the **Duke of Northumberland's family for over 700 years**.

But let's be honest—many visitors come here for one reason: **Harry Potter**. Alnwick Castle was famously used as **Hogwarts** in the first two films, and you can even take a broomstick-flying lesson on the very spot where Harry learned to soar!

Beyond its wizarding fame, Alnwick offers stunning medieval architecture, opulent state rooms, and the beautifully landscaped Alnwick Garden, home to the infamous Poison Garden, where every plant can kill you (yes, really).

Warkworth Castle: Medieval Legends and Hidden Hermitages

If you like your castles with a side of mystery, **Warkworth Castle** is the place to be. This **12th-century fortress**, perched on a loop of the River Coquet, is steeped in **medieval drama and intrigue**.

Once home to the powerful Percy family, Warkworth has seen its fair share of battles and betrayals. Wander through its imposing **Great Tower, explore the ancient chapel, and climb to the top for sweeping views** of the countryside.

Hidden nearby is the **Warkworth Hermitage**, a mysterious **medieval cave chapel carved into the**

rock, only accessible by boat. It's one of the most unique and tranquil spots in Northumberland.

Lindisfarne Castle & Holy Island: The Tidal Kingdom

There's something truly magical about **Lindisfarne**. Also known as **Holy Island**, this tidal island is home to **Lindisfarne Castle**, a 16th-century fortress perched atop a rocky hill, overlooking the North Sea.

What makes Lindisfarne special? The fact that **twice a day, it becomes completely cut off from the mainland** by the rising tide. It's an island steeped in history, from Viking raids to monastic life, and has an atmosphere like nowhere else.

Visitors can **walk the ancient causeway at low tide, explore the ruined Lindisfarne Priory, and sample the island's famous Lindisfarne Mead**, brewed by monks for centuries.

Dunstanburgh Castle: Ruins by the Sea

For sheer dramatic beauty, **Dunstanburgh Castle** is unbeatable. Unlike the well-preserved grandeur of Bamburgh or Alnwick, Dunstanburgh is a ruin—but what a ruin it is!

Perched on a rugged **headland overlooking the North Sea**, this **14th-century fortress** is accessible only by a stunning **coastal walk from the village of Craster**. The journey itself is worth the visit, with **cliffs, seabirds, and the occasional seal** along the way.

Once a symbol of power during England's turbulent Wars of the Roses, today Dunstanburgh is a hauntingly beautiful reminder of Northumberland's wild past.

These castles aren't just historic sites—they are stories carved in stone, waiting for you to step inside and experience their magic.

Northumberland's Natural Wonders

Northumberland National Park: A Hiker's Paradise

Covering over 400 square miles of breathtaking landscapes, Northumberland National Park is a dream for outdoor lovers. With rolling hills, deep valleys, and hidden waterfalls, the park offers some of the most stunning scenery in England. The Dark Sky Park status also makes it one of the best places in the UK for stargazing—on a clear night, the Milky Way stretches across the sky like a celestial river. Whether you prefer a gentle countryside stroll or a challenging hike up the Simonside Hills, this park has something for everyone.

For hikers, the Hadrian's Wall Path is a must, offering a mix of history and nature. If you're after a peaceful picnic spot, head to Hareshaw Linn, a magical woodland walk leading to a cascading waterfall. Birdwatchers will love the remote College Valley, a haven for rare birds like the hen harrier.

Recommendations:

- Best time to visit: Spring and summer for wildflowers and lush landscapes; autumn for golden hues.
- Where to stay: Try The Pheasant Inn in Kielder or the charming St. Cuthbert's House B&B.
- Nearby food stop: Visit The Kirkstyle Inn for hearty local dishes and real ale.

The Cheviot Hills: Climbing the Wild Frontier

If you're looking for a proper adventure, the Cheviot Hills deliver. This rugged mountain range straddles the border between England and Scotland, offering dramatic views and a sense of solitude that's hard to find elsewhere. The highest peak, The Cheviot, stands at 815 meters and rewards those who make the climb with sweeping panoramas that stretch as far as the eye can see. The landscape is dotted with ancient hillforts and remnants of Roman roads, adding a historical dimension to your trek.

Hiking here isn't for the faint-hearted—the terrain is boggy in places, and the weather can shift rapidly. But the rewards? Unparalleled views, an escape from crowds, and a true sense of wilderness. If you're lucky, you might even spot a golden eagle soaring overhead.

Recommendations:

- Best route: The Harthope Valley loop offers incredible scenery and a steady climb to the summit.
- Essential gear: Waterproof boots, layers, and a map—mobile signal is unreliable.
- Where to eat: The Red Lion Inn in Wooler serves up fantastic post-hike meals.

Kielder Water & Forest Park: The Largest Man-Made Lake in the UK

Kielder Water isn't just a lake—it's a vast, shimmering expanse that holds more water than all of the lakes in the Lake District combined. Surrounded by the largest working forest in England, this park is an outdoor playground where you can kayak across glassy waters, cycle along endless forest trails, or simply sit back and enjoy the peace and quiet.

Wildlife enthusiasts will be thrilled to know that Kielder is home to ospreys, red squirrels, and even the elusive otter. Visit Kielder Bird of Prey Centre for an up-close look at magnificent raptors. And when night falls, this area transforms into an astronomer's paradise—Kielder Observatory offers some of the best stargazing opportunities in Europe, far from the glare of city lights.

Recommendations:

- Best activities: Boat trips, forest cycling, and dark sky astronomy sessions.
- Family-friendly fun: The Kielder Water Birds of Prey Centre is great for kids.
- Where to stay: Kielder Waterside lodges provide stunning lake views and cozy comfort.

Farne Islands: A Seabird and Seal Sanctuary

A short boat ride off the Northumberland coast takes you to the Farne Islands, a wildlife haven where nature reigns supreme. These rocky islets are home to tens of thousands of seabirds, including puffins, guillemots, and Arctic terns. Watching the puffins waddle about with beaks full of fish is a sight straight out of a nature documentary. But the real stars of the show? The grey seals. The islands host one of the largest grey seal colonies in England, and if you visit in autumn, you'll see hundreds of adorable seal pups lounging on the shores.

If you're feeling adventurous, book a boat tour from Seahouses—options range from wildlife-watching trips to landings on Inner Farne, where you can walk among the nesting birds (but wear a hat, as the terns have a habit of dive-bombing visitors!).

Recommendations:

- Best time to visit: May to July for puffin season; September to November for seal pups.
- Best tour: Billy Shiel's Boat Trips offers excellent wildlife excursions.
- Where to eat: The Olde Ship Inn in Seahouses serves fantastic seafood with a view

Charming Towns & Villages

Alnwick: Market Town with a Storybook Charm

In the heart of Northumberland, Alnwick is a picture-perfect market town that feels like it's straight out of a fairy tale. The town's narrow cobbled streets are lined with independent shops, tea rooms, and historic pubs, making it a delightful place to stroll around. But the true magic of Alnwick lies in its grand castle—the home of the Duke of Northumberland. Alnwick Castle isn't just a place to admire from the outside; it's a living, breathing part of the town, steeped in history and brimming with stories.

Visitors flock here not only to admire the majestic architecture but also to immerse themselves in the very real history of the area. Alnwick's charm is truly its juxtaposition of old-world elegance and the everyday buzz of modern life. Plus, Harry Potter fans will recognize the castle from its role as Hogwarts in the first two films. If you're keen on a magical experience, be sure to explore the Alnwick Garden, a beautifully landscaped oasis, featuring a Poison Garden and the world's largest treehouse restaurant.

Recommendations:

- Best time to visit: Spring or summer, when the gardens are in full bloom.
- Don't miss: A walk around Alnwick Castle, especially the Harry Potter-themed broomstick training experience.
- Where to eat: The Treehouse Restaurant, located in Alnwick Garden, offers an unforgettable dining experience in the treetops.

PLEASE SCAN HERE TO VIEW MAP

Seahouses: A Gateway to the Farne Islands

A bustling coastal village, Seahouses is the quintessential gateway to the Farne Islands. Located just a stone's throw from the islands, this charming fishing village is packed with character. You can't miss the picturesque harbor where you'll find colorful boats bobbing in the water, ready to take you on a boat tour to see the seals and seabirds that make the Farne Islands so special.

Seahouses is also home to some great seafood restaurants, where you can enjoy the freshest catch of the day. One of the town's highlights is the Seahouses Lifeboat Station, which has been saving lives at sea for generations. For nature lovers and wildlife enthusiasts, Seahouses offers a wonderful mix of seaside charm and adventure.

Recommendations:

- Best time to visit: Summer for the best wildlife experiences, particularly from May to July when puffins are nesting.
- Must-do: A boat trip to the Farne Islands with Billy Shiel's Boat Trips for a close-up of the wildlife.

- Where to stay: The Bamburgh Castle Inn offers beautiful views over the harbor and is a great base for exploring the coastline.

PLEASE SCAN HERE TO VIEW MAP

Berwick-upon-Tweed: A Border Town with a Bloody Past

Straddling the border between England and Scotland, Berwick-upon-Tweed has been at the heart of centuries of conflict and cultural fusion. The town's turbulent past is still evident in its architecture, which reflects a blend of both English and Scottish styles. Berwick's star-shaped defensive walls and impressive military history make it a fascinating town to explore.

The town is also home to beautiful Georgian streets and peaceful riverside walks along the Tweed. Be sure to visit Berwick's Elizabethan Walls, which offer spectacular views of the town and the surrounding landscape. For a truly unique experience, make your way to the Berwick Barracks and Military Museum to learn about the town's strategic importance through history.

Recommendations:

- Best time to visit: Autumn when the town is less crowded, and the golden sunsets over the river are especially striking.
- Don't miss: A walk along the town's historic walls for panoramic views of the coastline.
- Where to eat: The Maltings Café, located near the Berwick Barracks, serves excellent locally-sourced dishes.

PLEASE SCAN HERE TO VIEW MAP

Rothbury & Cragside House: Victorian Innovation in Nature

Rothbury, a picturesque village nestled in the Coquet Valley, is a fantastic starting point for exploring the surrounding countryside. The village's charm lies in its mix of Georgian architecture, quaint shops, and lovely riverside walks. But it's the nearby Cragside House that truly steals the show.

Cragside House was once home to the Victorian inventor Lord Armstrong, and it is known for its innovative use of hydroelectric power, making it the first house in the world to be lit by electricity. The estate is a masterpiece of Victorian architecture and design, surrounded by acres of woodland and formal gardens. It's a place where history and nature beautifully collide. Be sure to explore the woodland walks, which are perfect for those who enjoy getting out into nature and experiencing some of the area's wildlife.

Recommendations:

- Best time to visit: Spring and summer, when the gardens are in full bloom and the weather is perfect for exploring.
- Don't miss: A tour of Cragside House, especially if you're interested in Victorian engineering and history.

- Where to stay: The Coquetdale Hotel in Rothbury offers a cozy base for exploring the village and surrounding countryside.

PLEASE SCAN HERE TO VIEW MAP

CHAPTER 3: THE NORTHUMBERLAND COAST – BEACHES, TRAILS & WILDLIFE

Northumberland's coast is a natural wonder, with its stunning beaches, scenic trails, and abundant wildlife. Whether you're a hiker, a beach lover, or a wildlife enthusiast, this stretch of coastline offers something for everyone. Let's dive in and explore the hidden gems and scenic beauty of Northumberland's coastline, which has remained relatively untouched by the modern world.

The Northumberland Coast Path: A Walk Through History and Nature

The Northumberland Coast Path is one of the UK's most scenic and rewarding walks. Stretching for 62 miles (100 km) from Cresswell in the south to Berwick-upon-Tweed in the north, this path takes you through some of the most breathtaking landscapes in England. The path winds along rugged cliffs, past golden sandy beaches, through charming villages, and alongside centuries of history, including ancient castles and tranquil harbors.

As you walk along the coast, you'll pass through the Farne Islands' views, which are teeming with seabirds and seals. The path offers a truly immersive experience, connecting you not only to the natural beauty of the region but also to its history. Along the way, you can stop and explore historic landmarks like Lindisfarne Castle, the medieval village of Craster, and the impressive ruins of Dunstanburgh Castle.

The path itself is relatively flat, making it suitable for walkers of all abilities, though some stretches along the cliffs can be more challenging. Regardless of your pace, the spectacular views over the North Sea and the coastline will keep you captivated.

Recommendations:

- Best time to visit: Spring and early autumn, when the weather is mild and the trails are less crowded.
- Must-do: Walk a portion of the path to experience both the history and natural beauty that Northumberland offers.

- Where to stay: There are numerous charming B&Bs and cottages along the route, such as those in the village of Beadnell.

Bamburgh Beach: Golden Sands Beneath a Mighty Castle

Bamburgh Beach is one of Northumberland's most iconic stretches of coastline, offering golden sands, dramatic dunes, and views of the magnificent Bamburgh Castle that rise like a sentinel above the beach. It's a place where history and nature collide, as you walk along the beach with the imposing castle towering overhead.

The beach itself is perfect for a relaxing walk, whether you're enjoying the fresh sea breeze or searching for seashells. Bamburgh Beach is known for its clean, soft sand, making it ideal for families, picnics, or simply soaking up the tranquility of the sea. It's also a popular spot for water sports, including surfing and kiteboarding, especially on a windy day.

After a day at the beach, take a short walk to the Bamburgh Castle, one of the most stunning castles in the country, perched on a rocky outcrop with sweeping views over the coastline. The castle itself is a fascinating place to explore, with its rich history, beautiful interiors, and expansive grounds.

Recommendations:

- Best time to visit: Summer, for pleasant weather and long days at the beach.
- Don't miss: A visit to Bamburgh Castle, one of the most iconic landmarks in Northumberland.
- Where to eat: The Copper Kettle Tea Room offers a delightful spot for lunch with great views of the castle.

Embleton Bay: A Photographer's Dream

Embleton Bay, often regarded as one of the most beautiful beaches in Northumberland, is a true photographer's paradise. The beach is framed by dramatic cliffs on one side and stretches of golden sand that seem to go on forever. The bay is surrounded by rugged dunes and is dotted with ancient stone formations, making it perfect for photography, especially at sunrise or sunset.

The beach is also home to the striking ruins of Dunstanburgh Castle, which stand on a headland overlooking the bay. The sight of the castle ruins against the backdrop of the sea and sky is unforgettable and provides ample opportunities for photographers to capture the beauty of the area.

The bay is quieter than some of the more tourist-heavy beaches in the area, making it ideal for a peaceful retreat. The crystal-clear waters and golden sand make it a perfect place for a relaxing day by the sea.

Recommendations:

- Best time to visit: Early morning or late afternoon for the best light and fewer crowds.
- Must-do: Take a walk to the ruins of Dunstanburgh Castle for amazing views of the bay and the surrounding coastline.
- Where to stay: Embleton has several charming cottages and local B&Bs, such as The Embleton House.

Druridge Bay: A Hidden Coastal Gem

Druridge Bay is one of Northumberland's hidden treasures. A long, unspoiled stretch of beach, it offers visitors a more tranquil alternative to some of the more popular beaches in the area. The beach is surrounded by sand dunes and a rich variety of birdlife, making it a paradise for nature lovers.

Druridge Bay is also a great spot for walking, running, or simply soaking in the natural beauty. The area is part of the Druridge Bay Country Park, which provides a combination of woodland, wetland, and beach environments. The park is also home to several bird hides, perfect for birdwatching enthusiasts.

The bay is ideal for a quiet picnic, with plenty of peaceful spots to relax and enjoy the view. Whether you're watching the waves crash against the shore or looking out for the seals that sometimes lounge on the beach, Druridge Bay feels like a secret sanctuary on the Northumberland coast.

Recommendations:

- Best time to visit: Spring and autumn for a peaceful escape and excellent birdwatching.
- Don't miss: A walk along the beach to enjoy the solitude and peace of the bay.
- Where to stay: The nearby village of Hadston offers several charming B&Bs.

PLEASE SCAN HERE TO VIEW MAP

Coquet Island: Puffins, Seals, and a Lighthouse

For those seeking a truly unforgettable wildlife experience, Coquet Island is a must-visit. This small, rugged island sits just off the coast of Amble and is home to a fascinating array of wildlife. The island is a sanctuary for puffins, which nest here in the summer months, and it is also home to large populations of seals and seabirds.

The island is managed by the RSPB, and while it's not open to the public, you can take a boat tour from Amble to see the island's wildlife up close. During the summer months, you can see puffins nesting along the cliffs, making it one of the best places in the UK to see these charming seabirds.

Coquet Island is also home to a historic lighthouse, which has been guiding ships safely along the coast since 1841. The sight of the lighthouse perched against the backdrop of the island's rugged cliffs is a classic photo opportunity for visitors.

Recommendations:

- Best time to visit: Summer, particularly June and July, when the puffins are nesting.
- Must-do: Take a boat tour from Amble to get close to the island and its wildlife.
- Where to stay: Amble has several charming guesthouses, such as The Harbour Guest House, which offers stunning views of the sea.

PLEASE SCAN HERE TO VIEW MAP

The Northumberland coast is one of the most scenic and diverse stretches of coastline in the UK. Whether you're walking the trails, relaxing on the beaches, or observing the wildlife, it offers endless opportunities to connect with nature and history. Plan your visit to this coastal paradise, and be prepared for a journey filled with breathtaking views and unforgettable experiences.

CHAPTER 5: ROMANTIC GETAWAYS – BEST PLACES FOR COUPLES

Northumberland is a paradise for couples seeking an unforgettable romantic escape. From luxurious retreats nestled in the countryside to charming hideaways by the coast, the county offers a variety of options to help you create special memories with your loved one. Whether you're looking to relax in a luxurious spa, indulge in gourmet dining, or enjoy scenic views of the countryside and coastline, Northumberland has the perfect romantic getaway for you.

Luxury Retreats with Stunning Views

Northumberland's tranquil landscape, with its rolling hills, rugged coastlines, and peaceful woodlands, offers an idyllic backdrop for couples seeking a luxurious and intimate retreat. The county is home to several high-end accommodations, each offering the perfect setting for a romantic escape. Let's explore some of the finest luxury retreats in Northumberland, each with its own charm, elegance, and unique offerings.

Doxford Hall Hotel & Spa: A Relaxing Country Escape

Tucked away in the heart of Northumberland, Doxford Hall Hotel & Spa is a luxurious country house hotel that exudes old-world charm and modern elegance. Set within 2,000 acres of beautiful parkland, this stunning estate offers a peaceful and intimate environment, making it a perfect destination for couples looking to unwind and reconnect.

The hotel's elegant interiors, including opulent rooms, a grand staircase, and romantic lounges, offer an atmosphere of sophistication and comfort. But what really sets Doxford Hall apart is its breathtaking grounds. Wander hand-in-hand through the manicured gardens, or take a leisurely stroll around the estate's lakes, where you can soak up the natural beauty of the countryside.

For couples seeking the ultimate relaxation, the hotel boasts a luxurious spa offering a range of treatments from massages to facials, ensuring you both leave feeling rejuvenated and pampered. There's also a fine dining restaurant, where you can enjoy a candlelit dinner made with fresh, local ingredients – perfect for a romantic evening.

Recommendations:

- Best for: Couples seeking relaxation, peace, and romance.
- Don't miss: A couple's spa treatment to unwind and rejuvenate together.
- Best time to visit: Year-round; however, spring and summer offer the added bonus of the stunning gardens in full bloom.
- Where to stay: Choose a room with a view of the parkland for a truly romantic setting.

Eshott Hall: A Hidden Gem for Romantic Stays

Nestled in the Northumberland countryside, Eshott Hall is an elegant Georgian mansion that provides a private and peaceful getaway for couples seeking a blend of luxury and tranquility. Eshott Hall is one of the county's best-kept secrets, a hidden gem offering a perfect blend of history, romance, and comfort.

The property itself is steeped in history, and its grand rooms feature antique furniture, original fireplaces, and beautiful wood paneling, creating a cozy and intimate atmosphere. The Hall's secluded position and stunning grounds provide an ideal setting for couples who want to escape from the world and enjoy a quiet, peaceful break.

Take a leisurely walk through the beautiful gardens or enjoy a picnic by the nearby lake, all while being surrounded by the beauty of nature. Eshott Hall also offers an outstanding dining experience with locally sourced dishes, perfect for a romantic meal for two. The intimate ambiance and exceptional service make it a favorite among couples celebrating anniversaries, engagements, or simply looking to spend quality time together.

Recommendations:

- Best for: Couples seeking a romantic and private retreat with a touch of history.
- Don't miss: A peaceful walk through the estate's grounds, particularly around the lake.
- Best time to visit: Spring, when the gardens are in full bloom, or autumn, when the surrounding woodland is ablaze with color.
- Where to stay: Opt for one of the luxurious four-poster bed rooms for a truly romantic experience.

These two luxurious retreats in Northumberland, Doxford Hall Hotel & Spa and Eshott Hall, offer couples the opportunity to experience romance in the tranquil beauty of the English countryside. Whether you're unwinding in a luxurious spa, dining by candlelight, or enjoying walks through scenic gardens, these retreats provide the ideal setting for an unforgettable romantic escape.

In Northumberland, there are endless opportunities for couples to create lasting memories, whether you prefer seclusion, luxury, or the natural beauty of the countryside.

Most Romantic Castles & Historic Spots

Northumberland's landscape is dotted with stunning castles and historic sites, many of which offer an air of mystery, romance, and timeless beauty. Whether you're strolling hand-in-hand along castle ruins at sunset or gazing over the wild coastline from a centuries-old fortress, these locations provide the perfect backdrop for a romantic escape.

Sunset Walks at Bamburgh Castle

Few places in England can match the dramatic beauty of **Bamburgh Castle**, perched high on a rocky crag overlooking the golden sands of Bamburgh Beach. With its imposing medieval walls and panoramic views of the North Sea, this castle is a dream setting for couples seeking both history and romance.

One of the most magical experiences at Bamburgh Castle is taking a **sunset walk** along the beach, watching as the sky transforms into hues of pink, orange, and purple while the castle stands proudly against the changing light. The soft sound of the waves, the fresh sea breeze, and the silhouette of the castle against the evening sky make for an unforgettable romantic moment.

For couples who enjoy a touch of history, explore the castle's grand halls, medieval artifacts, and fascinating tales of Northumberland's past. The castle's links to **the Victorian heroine Grace Darling**, who bravely rescued shipwrecked sailors in 1838, add an extra layer of romance to its storied past.

Recommendations:

- **Best for:** Couples who love coastal walks, stunning views, and historic charm.
- **Don't miss:** A picnic on the sand dunes just before sunset—bring a blanket and some wine for the perfect date night.
- **Best time to visit:** Spring and summer for longer daylight hours, but winter sunsets here are breathtaking too.
- **Where to stay:** Opt for a **cozy cottage in Bamburgh village**, or splurge on a stay at **The Victoria Hotel**, just a short walk from the castle.

Lindisfarne Castle: A Fairytale Setting on the Tides

If there's one place in Northumberland that feels like it belongs in a **storybook romance**, it's **Lindisfarne Castle**. Situated on **Holy Island**, this remote and enchanting fortress is surrounded by the shifting tides of the North Sea, making it feel almost otherworldly.

Unlike the grand fortresses of Bamburgh or Alnwick, Lindisfarne Castle is more **intimate and atmospheric**, perched on a rocky outcrop with spectacular views of the island and beyond. Walking up the winding path to the castle, with the wind in your hair and the sea stretching endlessly before you, feels like stepping into a romantic legend.

For couples seeking a secluded escape, Holy Island itself is the perfect retreat. The island is only accessible **at low tide via a causeway**, adding a touch of adventure to the experience. Spend the day exploring the **ancient priory ruins**, enjoying **fresh Lindisfarne Mead** at St. Aidan's Winery, and wandering the windswept beaches before heading up to the castle for an unforgettable sunset.

Recommendations:

- **Best for:** Couples who love history, island adventures, and magical landscapes.

- **Don't miss:** Checking the tide times before your visit—there's something thrilling about driving across the causeway knowing it will soon be swallowed by the sea.
- **Best time to visit:** Autumn is ideal for fewer crowds and crisp air, but summer offers stunning views with wildflowers blooming along the paths.
- **Where to stay:** Consider a romantic overnight stay at **The Manor House Hotel**, a charming retreat with views over the island.

Bamburgh Castle and Lindisfarne Castle are two of the most romantic spots in Northumberland, offering couples a perfect blend of **history, adventure, and breathtaking scenery**. Whether you're taking a sunset stroll along the beach, standing on a tidal island overlooking the waves, or simply enjoying the tranquility of these historic settings, these locations promise an unforgettable romantic escape.

Secluded Beaches for Couples

While Northumberland boasts some of the most breathtaking coastlines in England, some beaches remain blissfully untouched by the crowds. If you and your partner crave solitude, where the only sounds are the waves lapping against the shore and the distant calls of seabirds, these hidden gems are perfect for a romantic escape.

Howick Bay: A Quiet Coastal Escape

Tucked away between Craster and Boulmer, **Howick Bay** is a secluded stretch of coastline that remains one of Northumberland's best-kept secrets. Unlike the more famous Bamburgh Beach, Howick Bay is a place where you're more likely to encounter **seals basking on the rocks than other visitors**.

The beauty of Howick Bay lies in its **rugged, untouched charm**. With dramatic cliffs, rock pools teeming with marine life, and golden sand blending into shingle, the bay offers the perfect setting for a quiet afternoon away from the world. Take a **romantic walk along the coastal path**, explore the nearby **Howick Hall Gardens (home of Earl Grey tea!)**, or simply sit on the rocks and watch the waves roll in.

For adventurous couples, Howick Bay is also great for **wild swimming**, though be warned—the North Sea is refreshingly cool, even in summer!

Recommendations:

- **Best for:** Couples who love rugged landscapes and quiet, off-the-beaten-path locations.
- **Don't miss:** A visit to **Howick Hall Gardens & Arboretum**, where you can sip authentic **Earl Grey tea** in a charming tea room.

- **Best time to visit:** Late spring to early autumn, when the weather is mild, and the wildflowers along the cliffs are in full bloom.
- **Where to stay: Dunstanburgh Castle Hotel** in nearby Embleton offers cozy accommodations and easy access to the coastal path.

Sugar Sands Beach: A Hidden Paradise

Just south of Longhoughton, **Sugar Sands Beach** is the kind of place that feels like your own private paradise. The name itself evokes images of a soft, golden shoreline, and that's exactly what you'll find here. Accessible via a winding country lane and a short coastal walk, Sugar Sands is **remote enough to stay peaceful but rewarding enough to be worth the effort**.

The sheltered cove, framed by dramatic cliffs, makes it a **perfect spot for couples looking for a romantic seaside picnic**. The waters here are unusually **calm and clear**, making it one of the best spots in Northumberland for a refreshing dip—if you can brave the cold! The beach is also fantastic for **sunset watching**, as the colors reflect beautifully off the sea and the surrounding rocks.

What makes Sugar Sands even more special is the **sense of adventure** in getting there. Unlike the more accessible beaches, this one requires a bit of effort—but that only adds to the magic. If you and your partner love the idea of finding your own secret spot by the sea, this is the perfect destination.

Recommendations:

- **Best for:** Couples seeking a hidden, romantic beach away from crowds.
- **Don't miss:** Bringing a blanket and a picnic—there are no shops or facilities, just nature at its finest.
- **Best time to visit:** Summer is ideal for a beach day, but autumn adds an extra layer of tranquility with fewer visitors.
- **Where to stay:** Consider a stay at **The Joiners Arms** in Newton-by-the-Sea, a cozy boutique inn with rustic charm and excellent food.

Both **Howick Bay and Sugar Sands Beach** offer the kind of romantic, secluded setting that makes for an unforgettable getaway. Whether you prefer the **dramatic cliffs and history** of Howick Bay or the **hidden paradise** of Sugar Sands, these beaches promise a special escape where it feels like just the two of you, the sea, and the endless sky.

Best Restaurants for a Romantic Dinner

Northumberland is not just about castles and beaches—it also has some wonderful restaurants for a

romantic meal. Whether you want a **magical setting** or a **cozy spot by the sea**, these places are perfect for a special evening.

The Treehouse Restaurant at Alnwick Gardens

A Fairytale Dining Experience

Imagine eating dinner inside a **huge treehouse**, surrounded by **fairy lights, wooden walkways, and a warm fire**. That's exactly what you'll find at **The Treehouse Restaurant in Alnwick Gardens**—one of the most unique places to eat in Northumberland.

The inside is **cozy and romantic**, with wooden beams, soft lighting, and a real fire to keep you warm. The food is made with **fresh, local ingredients,** and the menu includes dishes like **grilled Northumbrian beef, fresh seafood, and creamy mushroom risotto.**

For drinks, they have a great selection of **wines and cocktails**, including their special **elderflower-infused "Forest Whisper" cocktail**.

If you want the **most romantic experience**, ask for a table **near the fire or outside under the lanterns**.

Tips:

- **Best for:** Couples who want a **magical, one-of-a-kind dining experience**.
- **Must-try dish: Grilled Northumbrian beef fillet** with a glass of red wine.
- **Best time to visit: Evening**, when the fairy lights make it feel truly magical.
- **Booking tip: Reserve a table in advance!** This place is very popular for romantic dates.

Potted Lobster, Bamburgh

Cozy Coastal Dining

If you love fresh seafood and a relaxed atmosphere, The Potted Lobster in Bamburgh is a perfect spot for a romantic dinner. Located just a short walk from Bamburgh Castle and the beach, this restaurant has a warm, intimate setting that's perfect for couples.

The menu focuses on locally caught seafood, with dishes like hand-dived scallops, fresh North Sea lobster, and beer-battered fish and chips. If seafood isn't your thing, they also offer delicious steaks and vegetarian options.

The atmosphere here is laid-back but stylish, with wooden tables, soft lighting, and friendly staff. It's the kind of place where you can relax, enjoy good food, and take your time.

Tips:

- **Best for:** Couples who love **great seafood in a relaxed setting**.
- **Must-try dish:** The **lobster thermidor** or the **pan-fried scallops**.
- **Best time to visit: Dinner time**, when you can enjoy a **romantic meal after a beach walk**.
- **Booking tip:** This place is **small and popular**, so it's best to **book ahead**, especially on weekends.

Both of these restaurants offer **a special experience**, whether you prefer **a magical treehouse setting** or **a cozy seafood spot by the coast**. Either way, you're sure to have **an unforgettable romantic evening** in Northumberland.

CHAPTER 6: SENIOR-FRIENDLY TRAVEL IN NORTHUMBERLAND

Northumberland is a **wonderful destination for seniors**, offering **stunning landscapes, fascinating history, and easy-to-explore attractions**. Whether you love **gentle walks, beautiful coastlines, or historic sites**, there's something here for you.

Easiest Walks with Stunning Views

Not all of Northumberland's landscapes require **steep climbs or long treks**. Here are some of the best

gentle walks with **beautiful views**, perfect for those who prefer **a slower pace**.

The Low-Level Walk at Hadrian's Wall

A Scenic Walk Through Roman History

Hadrian's Wall is one of the most famous landmarks in Northumberland, but you don't have to hike its toughest sections to enjoy it. The **low-level walks** near **Housesteads and Chesters Roman Forts** offer **stunning views of the countryside**, while keeping the terrain mostly **flat and easy to navigate**.

Along the way, you can take your time exploring **ancient ruins, old watchtowers, and scenic rolling hills**. Benches are available at certain points, so you can **pause, rest, and take in the views**.

Tips:

- **Best for:** History lovers who want **a gentle walk without steep climbs**.
- **Distance: 1 to 2 miles** (you can adjust based on your preference).
- **Best time to visit: Spring and autumn** for mild weather and fewer crowds.
- **Accessibility:** Some sections are **gravel paths**, but many are **well-maintained and easy to walk on**.

Coastal Paths with Benches and Rest Stops

Relaxing Walks Along Northumberland's Stunning Coast

If you prefer **sea views over Roman ruins**, Northumberland's **coastal paths** are a great option. These **gentle trails** take you along **golden beaches, charming villages, and rocky cliffs**, with plenty of **benches and rest areas** along the way.

Bamburgh to Seahouses Coastal Walk

This **flat and easy walk** follows the coastline between **Bamburgh and Seahouses**, offering **breathtaking views of Bamburgh Castle, the Farne Islands, and the North Sea**. The path is well-maintained, and there are **several spots to sit and rest**, making it ideal for seniors who want a **relaxed coastal stroll**.

Tips:

- **Best for:** A **gentle seaside walk** with **great castle views**.
- **Distance: About 3 miles**, but you can turn back whenever you like.
- **Best time to visit: Early morning or late afternoon** for **cooler temperatures and peaceful surroundings**.

- **Accessibility:** The path is **well-kept**, but some areas may be slightly sandy.

Alnmouth Estuary Walk

For a **short and easy riverside walk**, the **Alnmouth Estuary Trail** is a fantastic choice. It offers **peaceful views of the River Aln, charming boats, and a beautiful beach**, with **plenty of places to sit and relax**. The village of **Alnmouth** is also a lovely place to explore, with **tea rooms, art galleries, and a friendly atmosphere**.

Tips:

- **Best for:** A **quiet, relaxing riverside walk**.
- **Distance:** Around **1.5 miles**, making it **perfect for a slow stroll**.
- **Best time to visit: Midday**, when the light is beautiful and the cafes are open.
- **Accessibility: Mostly flat and easy to walk**, with some paved sections.

These **easy walking routes** allow seniors to **experience Northumberland's beauty** without the need for **steep climbs or long hikes**. Whether you choose a **historic Roman trail** or a **peaceful seaside walk**, you'll find plenty of **places to rest, admire the views, and soak in the beauty of Northumberland**.

Historic Sites with Easy Access

Northumberland is filled with **fascinating historic sites**, but not all of them require climbing steep hills or navigating rough terrain. Here are two **senior-friendly historic attractions** that offer **easy access, beautiful scenery, and a comfortable visiting experience**.

Alnwick Castle & Gardens (Mobility-Friendly)

A Grand Castle with Easy Exploration

Alnwick Castle is one of **Northumberland's most famous landmarks**, known for its **majestic architecture, rich history, and role in the Harry Potter films**. But beyond its cinematic fame, it's also **one of the best castles for seniors** thanks to its **mobility-friendly design**.

The castle grounds have **wide, well-maintained paths**, and there's **step-free access to most areas**. You can **stroll at a relaxed pace**, exploring **the grand courtyard, historic rooms, and exhibitions** without worrying about steep climbs.

Alnwick Garden: A Beautiful Escape

Next to the castle is the **Alnwick Garden**, an attraction in its own right. It features **a stunning Grand Cascade (a tiered water feature), a peaceful cherry orchard, and the famous Poison Garden**. The paths are **flat and well-paved**, making it easy to wander and enjoy the sights.

Recommendations:

- **Best for:** A relaxed **historic and garden experience**.
- **Accessibility:** **Wheelchair-friendly** and **step-free access available**.
- **Extra tip:** Book a **guided tour** to learn **fascinating history** with **minimal walking required**.
- **Don't Miss:** Afternoon tea at the Treehouse Restaurant, an enchanting spot with **woodland views**.

Cragside House: Beautiful Landscapes Without Strenuous Hiking

A Victorian Mansion with Stunning Views

Cragside House, once home to **Lord Armstrong**, is famous for being **the first house in the world powered by hydroelectricity**. Set in a beautiful forested estate, this mansion offers **history, innovation, and gorgeous scenery—all without requiring a tough hike**.

While Cragside's real estate has **steep woodland trails**, you don't need to take them to enjoy this **remarkable place**. The main house is **easily accessible**, and the formal gardens have **gentle paths where you can take in the beauty of the surroundings**.

Easy Ways to Explore Cragside

- **Take the Carriage Drive:** This **6-mile scenic drive** lets you enjoy the **best views of the estate** without having to walk long distances.
- **Visit the Rock Garden & Formal Gardens:** These areas have **gentle slopes and paved walkways**, making them easy to explore at a comfortable pace.
- **Relax in the Tea Room:** After your visit, enjoy a **cup of tea and homemade cake** in the **Cragside tea room**, offering a **cozy spot to rest with great views**.

Recommendations:

- **Best for: History lovers** who want a **scenic but easy-to-explore site**.

- **Accessibility:** The house is **mobility-friendly**, and the gardens have **flat paths** for a comfortable visit.
- **Extra tip:** If walking is a concern, use the **free shuttle service** between the visitor center and the house.

Both **Alnwick Castle & Gardens** and **Cragside House** offer **easy access, fascinating history, and stunning scenery** without the need for **strenuous walking**. Whether you want to **step into a medieval castle or explore a Victorian mansion**, these historic sites provide a **comfortable and enjoyable experience for seniors**.

Relaxing Activities for Seniors

Not every adventure in Northumberland requires **long walks or climbing hills**. If you prefer a **gentler pace**, there are plenty of **relaxing activities** that allow you to **soak in the region's beauty without too much effort**. Here are two of the best options:

Riverboat Cruises in Berwick-upon-Tweed

A Gentle Journey Through History and Nature

Berwick-upon-Tweed, **Northumberland's northernmost town**, is rich in history and set along the beautiful **River Tweed**. One of the most enjoyable ways to experience it is by taking a **leisurely riverboat cruise**.

Aboard a **comfortable sightseeing boat**, you'll glide past **historic bridges, medieval walls, and picturesque countryside** while listening to **fascinating stories about Berwick's past**. These cruises are **slow-paced, relaxing, and perfect for soaking up the scenery**.

Why Seniors Will Love It:

- **No walking required**—just sit back and enjoy the ride.
- **Great photo opportunities** of Berwick's famous **Royal Border Bridge** and riverside wildlife.
- **Friendly guides** who share **entertaining stories** about the town's **turbulent history**.

Recommendations:

- **Best for:** History lovers and nature enthusiasts who want a **calm, scenic experience**.
- **Accessibility:** Boats are **senior-friendly**, with easy boarding and comfortable seating.
- **Extra tip:** Bring a **light jacket**—the river breeze can be cool, even in summer.

Scenic Train Rides Through Northumberland

Sit Back and Enjoy the Countryside

If you love **breathtaking landscapes but prefer to avoid long walks**, a **scenic train journey** is the perfect way to experience Northumberland's beauty.

The **East Coast Main Line** runs **through Northumberland**, offering **unforgettable views** of **rolling hills, dramatic coastlines, and historic landmarks**. One of the most beautiful routes is between **Newcastle and Edinburgh**, which passes through **Alnmouth, Berwick-upon-Tweed, and the Holy Island coastline**.

What to Expect on the Journey:

- **Comfortable seating** and **large windows** for **panoramic countryside views**.
- Views of **Bamburgh Castle, Lindisfarne, and the Farne Islands** from the train.
- **Minimal effort required**—just **relax, enjoy a cup of tea, and watch the scenery roll by**.

Recommendations:

- **Best for:** Anyone who wants a **stress-free way to see Northumberland's highlights**.

- **Accessibility:** Trains have **step-free access, priority seating, and onboard restrooms**.
- **Extra tip:** Sit on the **right-hand side of the train** (heading north) for **the best coastal views**.

Both **riverboat cruises in Berwick-upon-Tweed** and **scenic train rides through Northumberland** offer a **peaceful way to explore** without the need for **long walks or physical effort**. Whether you want to **float along a historic river or ride through stunning landscapes**, these **senior-friendly activities** guarantee a **memorable and relaxing experience**.

Best Accommodations for Comfort & Accessibility

Finding the right place to stay is crucial for a stress-free trip, especially if you prefer comfort, accessibility, and convenience. Whether you're looking for a hotel with modern amenities or a cozy cottage close to attractions, Northumberland offers plenty of senior-friendly options.

Hotels with Elevators & Step-Free Access

Where Comfort Meets Convenience

Many historic hotels in Northumberland have been modernized to include step-free access, elevators, and accessible rooms. Here are some of the best choices for a comfortable and easy stay:

1. The Cookie Jar, Alnwick

Why You'll Love It:

- Located in the heart of Alnwick, just steps from Alnwick Castle & Gardens.
- Ground-floor rooms available for easy access.
- Offers luxurious but cozy decor, plus a quiet library lounge for relaxation.

2. Matfen Hall, near Hadrian's Wall

Why You'll Love It:

- A grand country hotel with an elevator and step-free access to key areas.
- Surrounded by stunning gardens—perfect for a gentle stroll.
- Has an award-winning spa, ideal for unwinding after a day of sightseeing.

3. Doxford Hall Hotel & Spa

Why You'll Love It:

- Traditional elegance with modern accessibility features, including a lift.
- Tranquil countryside location with beautiful walking paths.

- On-site spa and fine dining for a relaxing stay.

Cozy Cottages with Easy Walking Distance to Attractions

For those who prefer a more private and home-like stay, Northumberland has a range of charming cottages designed with accessibility in mind.

1. Budle Bay Bothy, Bamburgh

Why You'll Love It:

- A stylish single-story cottage with an open-plan design.
- Located near the beach and Bamburgh Castle.
- Wheelchair-friendly layout with no steps.

2. Market Cross Guest House, Belford

Why You'll Love It:

- A small but elegant guest house with ground-floor rooms.
- Easy access to local markets, cafes, and historical sites.
- A welcoming atmosphere with excellent personal service.

3. The Old School, Seahouses

Why You'll Love It:

- A former school turned into a beautiful and accessible holiday home.
- Walking distance to the harbor and boat trips to the Farne Islands.
- Equipped with wide doorways and a walk-in shower.

These accommodations ensure that seniors can **enjoy Northumberland with ease and comfort**, whether exploring historic castles, relaxing by the sea, or indulging in the region's finest cuisine.

CHAPTER 7: FOOD & DRINK IN NORTHUMBERLAND

Northumberland's food scene is a delightful mix of traditional flavors, fresh local ingredients, and historic culinary influences. Whether you're sampling smoky Craster kippers, indulging in a warm stottie cake, or sipping on the famous Lindisfarne mead, this chapter will guide you to the best dishes and dining spots across the county.

Traditional Northumbrian Dishes You Must Try

Craster Kippers: The Smoky Delight

If you visit Northumberland and don't try Craster Kippers, have you really been to Northumberland? These **oak-smoked herrings** are famous across Britain, with a deep, rich flavor that pairs beautifully with buttered toast. The best place to try them is **L. Robson & Sons in Craster**, where they've been perfecting the art of smoking fish for over a century.

Where to Try It:

- **The Jolly Fisherman, Craster** – Serves Craster kippers in a delicious breakfast dish.
- **L. Robson & Sons Smokehouse, Craster** – Buy some fresh to take home.

Stottie Cake: A Northumbrian Classic

Despite its name, a stottie isn't a cake—it's a **thick, doughy bread** baked to perfection and often filled with ham and pease pudding. It's the ultimate **hearty Northumbrian snack** and a must-try for anyone wanting a taste of local life.

Where to Try It:

- **Greggs (various locations)** – The North East's favorite bakery chain.
- **The Running Fox, Felton** – A cozy café known for its fresh-baked stotties.

Pan Haggerty: A Local Comfort Food

Think of pan haggerty as **Northumberland's answer to gratin potatoes**. It's a **layered dish of potatoes, onions, and cheese**, cooked to crispy perfection. Traditionally, it was a cheap and filling meal for miners, but today, it's a beloved regional classic.

Where to Try It:

- **The Potted Lobster, Bamburgh** – Serves a gourmet version with local cheese.
- **The Black Bull, Corbridge** – Traditional, home-cooked pan haggerty.

The Best Seafood Restaurants & Pubs

With a long coastline and a strong fishing heritage, Northumberland boasts some of the **freshest seafood in the UK**. Here are the best spots to indulge:

- **The Potted Lobster, Bamburgh** – Known for fresh lobster and seafood platters.

- **The Jolly Fisherman, Craster** – Amazing Craster kippers and seafood chowder.
- **Riley's Fish Shack, Tynemouth** – A rustic, beachfront spot for grilled seafood.
- **The Fish Shack, Amble** – A hidden gem for locally caught fish and chips.

Where to Try Lindisfarne Mead

Lindisfarne Mead is a **sweet, honey-infused wine**, said to have been enjoyed by monks on Holy Island for centuries. It's the perfect drink to sip while watching the tides roll in.

Best Places to Try & Buy:

- **St. Aidan's Winery, Lindisfarne** – The official mead producers on Holy Island.
- **The Mead Hall, Alnwick** – Offers tastings of various mead flavors.

Northumberland's Best Tea Rooms & Cafés

After a long walk along the coast or through the countryside, there's nothing better than **a warm cup of tea and a homemade scone**. Northumberland has some incredible tea rooms, often housed in historic buildings or cozy countryside settings.

Top Tea Rooms to Visit:

- **The Running Fox, Felton** – Famous for its **giant afternoon teas** and fresh-baked bread.
- **Earl Grey Tea House, Howick** – Set in the gardens of the **Earl Grey family estate**.
- **The Copper Kettle, Bamburgh** – A charming spot near Bamburgh Castle with homemade cakes.
- **Pilgrims Coffee House, Holy Island** – Great coffee and fresh bakes, with views of Lindisfarne.

From traditional **Northumbrian dishes** to award-winning **seafood and historic drinks**, the county is full of **culinary surprises**. Whether you're indulging in a **cozy afternoon tea**, a **hearty meal in a country pub**, or a **fresh seafood feast**, Northumberland's food scene will leave you coming back for more.

CHAPTER 8: WHERE TO STAY – ACCOMMODATION FOR EVERY TRAVELER

Northumberland offers a variety of **accommodation options** to suit different budgets and travel styles. Whether you're looking for **a luxurious castle stay, a budget-friendly guesthouse, a cozy countryside retreat, or a unique glamping experience**, there's something for everyone. Below is an overview of some of the best places to stay, including locations and estimated costs where available.

Luxury Stays: Castle Hotels & Boutique Inns

For those looking for a high-end, historic, and romantic experience, Northumberland has some of England's most breathtaking castle hotels and boutique inns. These accommodations often include fine dining, stunning gardens, spa facilities, and grand interiors.

1. Langley Castle Hotel (Hexham) – A 14th-century castle hotel with four-poster beds, medieval décor, and gourmet dining. This hotel is perfect for a romantic getaway or a historical experience.

- **Cost:** From **£200–£400 per night**
- **Best For:** Couples, history lovers

2. Doxford Hall Hotel & Spa (Chathill) – A luxurious country house hotel with an indoor pool, full-service spa, and award-winning dining. The peaceful gardens and countryside views make it an excellent retreat for relaxation.

- **Cost:** From **£180–£350 per night**
- **Best For:** Spa weekends, relaxing getaways

3. Eshott Hall (Morpeth) – A hidden gem in the Northumberland countryside, offering elegant rooms, fine dining, and a peaceful atmosphere. This Georgian mansion is ideal for quiet retreats and special occasions.

- **Cost:** From **£150–£300 per night**
- **Best For:** Romantic escapes, food lovers

4. Walwick Hall (Hexham) – A luxury boutique hotel near Hadrian's Wall, offering modern comfort in a countryside setting. It features a spa, fine dining, and elegant rooms with stunning views.

- **Cost:** From **£220–£400 per night**
- **Best For:** Relaxing breaks, couples, history enthusiasts

5. Matfen Hall (Near Newcastle) – A beautiful country manor with a championship golf course, spa, and fine dining. The grand architecture and tranquil surroundings make it perfect for leisurely stays.

- **Cost:** From **£190–£380 per night**
- **Best For:** Golfers, luxury seekers

Budget-Friendly Guesthouses & Hostels

If you're looking for **affordable yet comfortable accommodation**, Northumberland has **many budget-friendly guesthouses and hostels** with great locations.

1. YHA The Sill at Hadrian's Wall (Hexham) – A modern **youth hostel** offering **affordable dorm beds and private rooms**, perfect for travelers exploring **Hadrian's Wall**.

- **Cost:** From £25 per night (dorm), £50 per night (private room)
- **Best For:** Hikers, backpackers

2. The Roxburgh (Spittal, Berwick-upon-Tweed)
– A cozy **seaside guesthouse** with **comfortable rooms and beautiful sea views** at a budget price.

- **Cost:** From **£50–£80 per night**
- **Best For:** Budget travelers, coastal explorers

3. No.1 Hotel & Wine Lounge (Wooler) – A charming, affordable **guesthouse with a warm atmosphere** and a cozy **wine bar**.

- **Cost:** From **£70–£120 per night**
- **Best For:** Budget travelers, couples

4. Beach Court (Seahouses) – A small **family-run guesthouse** near the harbor, perfect for **exploring the Northumberland coast**.

- **Cost:** From **£60–£100 per night**
- **Best For:** Solo travelers, coastal walkers

5. Castle Vale House B&B (Berwick-upon-Tweed) – A budget-friendly bed and breakfast with Victorian charm and great views of the River Tweed.

- **Cost:** From **£65–£110 per night**
- **Best For:** Travelers on a budget, history lovers

Cozy Cottages & Self-Catering Retreats

For those who prefer **a home-away-from-home experience**, **self-catering cottages** offer privacy, space, and the chance to immerse in Northumberland's beautiful countryside.

1. The Old Bakery (Alnwick) – A **charming cottage** in the heart of **Alnwick**, close to the **castle, gardens, and markets**.

- **Cost:** From **£90–£150 per night**
- **Best For:** Families, couples

2. Seahouses Cottage (Seahouses) – A **coastal cottage** perfect for those wanting to **explore the Farne Islands and Bamburgh Castle**.

- **Cost:** From **£85–£140 per night**
- **Best For:** Families, groups

3. Tosson Tower Farm Cottages (Rothbury) – A **rural retreat with stunning countryside views**, ideal for **hikers and nature lovers**.

- **Cost:** From **£80–£160 per night**
- **Best For:** Nature lovers, peace seekers

4. **Beacon Hill Farm (Morpeth)** – A collection of **luxury self-catering lodges** set on a private **farm estate with a spa and swimming pool**.

- **Cost:** From **£100–£180 per night**
- **Best For:** Longer stays, families

5. **Haven Cottages (Beadnell Bay)** – A **beachfront cottage with spectacular sea views**, perfect for **summer vacations**.

- **Cost:** From **£100–£170 per night**
- **Best For:** Beach lovers, families

Unique Stays: Glamping, Yurts & Farmstays

For a **memorable stay in nature**, Northumberland offers unique **glamping pods, yurts, and farm experiences** where you can **sleep under the stars, wake up to the sounds of wildlife, and enjoy a rustic escape**.

1. **Hesleyside Huts (Bellingham)** – Luxury **shepherd's huts and tree houses** with wood-burning stoves and stunning countryside views.

- **Cost:** From **£130–£250 per night**
- **Best For:** Couples, nature lovers

2. Wild Northumberland Glamping (Hexham) – Cozy **glamping pods with fire pits**, perfect for an **outdoor adventure with comfort**.

- **Cost:** From **£90–£150 per night**
- **Best For:** Glamping enthusiasts, couples

3. Alnwick Treehouse Glamping (Alnwick) – A **magical treehouse experience** near **Alnwick Castle and Gardens**.

- **Cost:** From **£160–£300 per night**
- **Best For:** Families, romantic getaways

4. Bamburgh Under Canvas (Bamburgh) – A **luxury camping experience** with **bell tents, cozy beds, and fire pits** near Bamburgh Beach.

- **Cost:** From **£80–£140 per night**
- **Best For:** Adventure seekers, couples

5. Laverock Law Cottages & Glamping (Lowick) – A **farmstay experience** where guests can interact with animals and enjoy the **peaceful countryside**.

- **Cost:** From **£85–£150 per night**
- **Best For:** Families, nature lovers

CHAPTER 9: FAMILY-FRIENDLY NORTHUMBERLAND

Northumberland is an **incredible destination for families**, offering a blend of **history, wildlife, outdoor adventures, and stunning beaches**. Whether your family enjoys **exploring medieval castles, meeting adorable animals, or playing on golden sandy beaches**, there's something for everyone. Below is a **detailed guide** to the best **family-friendly attractions** in Northumberland, complete with locations, activities, facilities, and costs.

Best Attractions for Kids

1. The Alnwick Garden & Treehouse (Alnwick)

Alnwick Garden is a fantasy-like playground for kids and adults alike. It features interactive water fountains, a giant treehouse restaurant, and unique themed gardens that will keep children entertained for hours. One of the highlights is the Poison Garden, where guides take families on a tour to see some of the world's most toxic plants—an educational yet thrilling experience.

- **Best For:** Families with kids of all ages
- **Activities:**
    - Playing in the water fountains
    - Exploring the Bamboo Labyrinth
    - Visiting the spooky Poison Garden
    - Dining in the enchanting Treehouse Restaurant
- **Facilities:** Café, gift shop, restrooms, picnic areas
- **Entry Fee:** £14 per adult, £7 per child

2. Kielder Water & Forest Park (Kielder)

This nature lover's paradise is home to the largest man-made lake in Northern Europe. Families can go cycling, hiking, wildlife spotting, and even stargazing in this officially designated Dark Sky Park. The adventure playgrounds, wildlife hides, and family-friendly bike trails make it a must-visit for those who love the outdoors.

- **Best For:** Outdoor-loving families, young explorers
- **Activities:**
    - Wildlife spotting (red squirrels, otters, birds of prey)
    - Cycling and walking trails
    - Stargazing at Kielder Observatory
    - Canoeing and kayaking on the lake
- **Facilities:** Parking, restrooms, picnic areas, café
- **Entry Fee:** Free (some activities may have an additional cost)

3. Whitehouse Farm Centre (Morpeth)

One of Northumberland's best farm attractions, Whitehouse Farm offers hands-on experiences where kids can feed and interact with alpacas, goats, rabbits, and guinea pigs. There are also tractor rides, outdoor play areas, and reptile encounters to keep children entertained.

- **Best For:** Families with toddlers and young children
- **Activities:**
    - Petting and feeding farm animals
    - Pony rides
    - Tractor-trailer rides
    - Indoor and outdoor play areas
- **Facilities:** Café, gift shop, picnic areas, restrooms
- **Entry Fee:** £13 per adult, £12 per child

4. Ford & Etal Estates (Near Berwick-upon-Tweed)

A perfect countryside escape for families, this estate offers a mix of heritage sites, a steam railway, a medieval castle, and an old-fashioned corn mill. Children will love riding the **Heatherslaw Light Railway**, a miniature train that runs through scenic landscapes.

- **Best For:** Families who love history and trains
- **Activities:**
    - Riding the Heatherslaw Light Railway
    - Exploring Etal Castle
    - Learning about milling at Heatherslaw Corn Mill
    - Visiting Hay Farm Heavy Horse Centre
- **Facilities:** Free parking, restrooms, picnic areas, café
- **Entry Fee:** Free entry (some attractions have a small fee)

5. Bailiffgate Museum & Gallery (Alnwick)

This small but engaging museum makes learning fun for children. It features interactive exhibits about Viking history, medieval knights, and local traditions. Kids can even dress up as knights and explore the replica medieval village.

- **Best For:** Families with school-aged children
- **Activities:**
    - Dressing up in medieval costumes
    - Exploring Viking history exhibits

- - Learning about Northumberland's past in a hands-on way
- **Facilities:** Gift shop, restrooms, baby-changing facilities
- **Entry Fee:** £5 per adult, £2 per child

Wildlife Parks & Farm Experiences

1. Northumberland Zoo (Felton)

A family-friendly zoo featuring snow leopards, meerkats, lynxes, and birds of prey. There are also hands-on animal feeding sessions and an indoor play area.

- **Best For:** Animal-loving families
- **Activities:**
  - Watching daily feeding sessions
  - Meeting exotic animals up close
  - Exploring the indoor play barn
- **Facilities:** Café, gift shop, picnic area, restrooms
- **Entry Fee:** £12 per adult, £10 per child

Interactive Castle Experiences for Families

1. Alnwick Castle (Alnwick)

Famous for its Harry Potter connections, this castle offers broomstick lessons, medieval workshops, and live performances.

- **Best For:** Families with kids who love fantasy
- **Activities:**
    - Broomstick flying lessons
    - Medieval archery
    - Knight's Quest (interactive role-playing area)
- **Entry Fee:** £19 per adult, £10 per child

Best Beaches for a Family Day Out

1. **Druridge Bay Beach**

A **long, sandy beach** with **safe shallow waters, picnic spots, and gentle waves**—ideal for younger children.

- **Best For:** Families with young kids
- **Activities:**
    - Sandcastle building
    - Rock pooling
    - Picnic by the sea
- **Facilities:** Free parking, toilets, café

2. Beadnell Bay

A **calm, sheltered bay** perfect for **paddleboarding, rock pooling, and family picnics**.

- **Best For:** Families who love beach activities
- **Activities:**
    - Paddleboarding and kayaking
    - Exploring rock pools
- **Facilities:** Toilets, parking, nearby shops

3. Seahouses Beach

A **great beach for boat trips to the Farne Islands, where kids can spot seals and puffins**.

- **Best For:** Families who love wildlife and boat trips
- **Activities:**
    - Wildlife watching (seals and puffins)
    - Sand dune exploration
- **Facilities:** Cafés, shops, parking

4. Bamburgh Beach

A **scenic beach with the backdrop of Bamburgh Castle**, ideal for **kite flying and beach games**.

- **Best For:** Families who love scenic beaches
- **Activities:**
    - Flying kites

- Exploring rock pools
- **Facilities:** Toilets, parking, dog-friendly

5. Sugar Sands Beach

A **hidden gem with soft golden sand and shallow water**, perfect for a **quiet family beach day**.

- **Best For:** Families who prefer secluded beaches
- **Activities:**
  - Swimming in shallow waters
  - Beachcombing
- **Facilities:** Limited parking, bring your own supplies

Northumberland is a fantastic family destination, offering castles filled with adventure, interactive wildlife experiences, and beautiful beaches for relaxation. Whether your family loves exploring medieval history, getting up close with animals, or enjoying coastal fun, Northumberland provides an unforgettable family getaway.

CHAPTER 10: HIDDEN GEMS & OFF-THE-BEATEN-PATH ADVENTURES

Northumberland isn't just about **famous castles and well-trodden hiking trails**—it's also home to **hidden gems** that many visitors never discover. From **secret waterfalls and remote villages** to **ancient stone circles and forgotten ruins**, this chapter unveils the **lesser-known** side of Northumberland, perfect for those who love **adventure and solitude**.

The Secret Waterfalls of Northumberland

1. Hareshaw Linn Waterfall (Near Bellingham)

A hidden woodland oasis, Hareshaw Linn is a beautiful 30-foot waterfall tucked away in a lush green valley. The trail leading to the waterfall takes you through **ancient woodland, over six bridges, and past rare wildlife** such as red squirrels and woodpeckers.

- **Why Visit?** A peaceful, fairy-tale setting with a rewarding view at the end
- **How to Get There:** A 3-mile round trip walk from Bellingham town center
- **Best Time to Visit:** Spring and autumn for the best water flow and vibrant foliage
- **Difficulty:** Easy to moderate (some uneven terrain)
- **Facilities:** Free parking in Bellingham, cafés nearby

2. Linhope Spout (Near Ingram Valley)

One of Northumberland's best-kept secrets, Linhope Spout is a 60-foot waterfall that plunges into a deep pool—perfect for a refreshing wild swim. The remote setting and surrounding moorland make it an incredible off-the-grid adventure.

- **Why Visit?** A stunning, secluded spot with a natural plunge pool
- **How to Get There:** A 3-mile walk from Hartside Farm near Ingram
- **Best Time to Visit:** Summer for wild swimming, autumn for dramatic water flow
- **Difficulty:** Moderate (some steep sections)

- **Facilities:** No facilities—pack everything you need

3. Hindhope Linn (Kielder Forest)

This **hidden waterfall** is located deep within **Kielder Forest**, making it one of the most **secluded and peaceful spots** in Northumberland. The short but scenic walk to the falls is lined with **towering trees, mossy rocks, and tranquil streams**.

- **Why Visit?** A quiet, enchanted woodland experience
- **How to Get There:** A 1.5-mile circular walk from Blakehope Burn Haugh car park
- **Best Time to Visit:** After heavy rain for the best waterfall flow
- **Difficulty:** Easy (flat terrain, but can be muddy)
- **Facilities:** Parking available, no nearby cafés

Remote Villages with Stunning Views

1. Alwinton

A **tiny village at the gateway to the Cheviot Hills**, Alwinton is perfect for those seeking **tranquility, incredible views, and historic charm**. It's surrounded by rolling hills, making it a fantastic spot for **hiking and stargazing**.

- **What's Special?** One of the best places in Northumberland for stargazing
- **Nearby Attractions:** Clennell Hall Country House, Kidland Forest

- **Best For:** Hikers, nature lovers, and those seeking solitude

2. Harbottle

Nestled in the **Coquet Valley**, Harbottle is home to the **dramatic ruins of Harbottle Castle** and the unique **Drake Stone**, a massive rock believed to have **healing powers**.

- **What's Special?** Mystical landscapes and great hiking trails
- **Nearby Attractions:** Harbottle Castle, Drake Stone
- **Best For:** History lovers, photographers, and adventurers

3. Blanchland

Built from **stone taken from a medieval abbey**, Blanchland is a **storybook village** that looks like something out of a movie. The **historic houses, riverside walks, and cozy pubs** make it one of Northumberland's most beautiful hidden spots.

- **What's Special?** A medieval village untouched by time
- **Nearby Attractions:** Derwent Reservoir, Blanchland Abbey
- **Best For:** Relaxing weekend getaways, history lovers

The Mysterious Duddo Stone Circle

Duddo Five Stones (Near Berwick-upon-Tweed)

Often referred to as Northumberland's Stonehenge, Duddo Stone Circle is a 5,000-year-old monument shrouded in mystery. Unlike the famous sites in England, Duddo's **quiet, remote setting** makes it feel truly **ancient and untouched**.

- **Why Visit?** A mystical and atmospheric place with stunning panoramic views
- **How to Get There:** A 1-mile walk from the small village of Duddo
- **Best Time to Visit:** Sunset or sunrise for an unforgettable experience
- **Difficulty:** Easy (gentle walk across fields)
- **Facilities:** None—bring water and snacks

Lesser-Known Ruins & Historic Sites

1. Edlingham Castle (Near Alnwick)

A ruined medieval manor house, Edlingham Castle is a hidden historic gem set against the backdrop of the Cheviot Hills. It's an off-the-beaten-path alternative to Northumberland's more famous castles.

- **What's Special?** A picturesque ruin with no crowds
- **Best For:** Photographers, history lovers
- **Entry Fee:** Free

2. Warkworth Hermitage (Warkworth)

A truly unique and hidden attraction, Warkworth Hermitage is a medieval chapel carved directly into a rock face. It's only accessible by boat, adding to the adventure.

- **What's Special?** A secret chapel hidden inside a cliff
- **Best For:** History buffs, adventurers
- **Entry Fee:** £5 per person (includes boat ride)

3. Brinkburn Priory (Near Rothbury)

A stunning medieval priory hidden in a peaceful wooded valley, Brinkburn Priory is perfect for those who love history and solitude. The Gothic architecture and riverside setting make it a tranquil escape.

- **What's Special?** A secluded medieval priory in a picturesque setting
- **Best For:** History lovers, photographers
- **Entry Fee:** £6 per adult, free for children under 5

CHAPTER 11: EVENTS & FESTIVALS IN NORTHUMBERLAND 2025

Northumberland is alive with **festivals and events** throughout the year, celebrating its **music, art, heritage, food, and countryside traditions**. Whether you're into **live music, film, historical reenactments, or family-friendly fun**, there's something for everyone.

Alnwick International Music Festival

- **When:** Early August 2025

- **Where:** Alnwick Market Square

- **What to Expect:** A vibrant celebration of **folk music and dance** featuring performers from around the world. Expect a mix of **traditional British, European, and global music styles**, with everything from Scottish bagpipes to Spanish flamenco.

- **Highlights:**

    - **Free daily performances** in Alnwick Market Square
    - A **parade of international musicians and dancers**
    - Opportunities to try **local street food** and traditional Northumbrian dishes
    - Workshops where visitors can learn **folk dance steps**
- **Who Should Go?** Music lovers, culture enthusiasts, and families looking for an **authentic, global festival atmosphere** in the heart of Northumberland.

- **Top Tip:** Arrive early to get a good spot in the **Market Square**, and explore **Alnwick Castle and Gardens** while you're in town.

The Berwick Film & Media Arts Festival

- **When:** September 2025

- **Where:** Various venues across Berwick-upon-Tweed

- **What to Expect:** One of the UK's most innovative film festivals, the Berwick Film & Media Arts Festival showcases **cutting-edge films, documentaries, and media installations** in unique historic settings, including **old barracks, medieval towers, and churches**.

- **Highlights:**

    - Screenings of **independent films and documentaries** from around the world
    - Outdoor film projections on **Berwick's medieval walls**
    - **Artist talks, workshops, and panel discussions** on film and media
    - A chance to explore **experimental film and digital art installations**

- **Who Should Go?** Film buffs, artists, and those interested in **independent cinema and** creative storytelling.

- **Top Tip:** Book tickets in advance for the **most popular screenings**, and take a walk along **Berwick's historic walls** for stunning views of the River Tweed.

Northumberland County Show

- **When:** Late May 2025

- **Where:** Bywell, near Corbridge

- **What to Expect:** Northumberland's **biggest agricultural event**, where you can experience the **best of rural life**, from **prize-winning livestock** to traditional craft displays. Perfect for families and anyone who loves the countryside.

- **Highlights:**
  - **Livestock competitions** featuring cattle, sheep, and horses
  - **Sheepdog trials** and falconry displays
  - **Local food and drink stalls** showcasing Northumberland produce

- - **Vintage vehicle displays** and tractor rides
  - **Family-friendly activities**, including fairground rides and craft workshops
- **Who Should Go?** Families, countryside lovers, and anyone interested in **farming, food, and rural traditions**.

- **Top Tip:** Wear comfortable shoes, as the showground is **large and mostly grassy**. Try a **Craster Kipper sandwich** from one of the food stalls!

Kielder Winter Wonderland

- **When:** Late November – December 2025

- **Where:** Kielder Forest

- **What to Expect:** A magical **Christmas-themed event** in the heart of Kielder Forest, featuring festive activities, a **Santa's grotto**, and stunning **woodland lights displays**.

- **Highlights:**

- Meet **Santa and his reindeer** in an enchanting forest setting
- **Interactive workshops**, including gingerbread making and Christmas crafts
- **Illuminated winter trails** through Kielder's magical woodland
- **Festive storytelling sessions** and live Christmas performances
- **Snow play areas** (with artificial snow, just in case!)

- **Who Should Go?** Families, Christmas lovers, and anyone looking for a **magical winter experience**.

- **Top Tip:** Kielder is **remote and can be very cold in winter**—wrap up warm, and book tickets early as this event sells out fast.

From music and film festivals to countryside fairs and winter wonderlands, Northumberland's events calendar is packed with exciting celebrations. Whether you're visiting in summer for outdoor music and film screenings, or in winter for Christmas magic in Kielder, there's always something special happening in Northumberland.

CHAPTER 12: PRACTICAL TRAVEL TIPS & FINAL THOUGHTS

Northumberland is a land of rugged coastlines, historic castles, charming villages, and unspoiled nature. To make the most of your trip, it's essential to plan ahead, pack wisely, and travel responsibly. This chapter will guide you through what to bring, how to stay safe, and how to protect the beauty of this incredible region.

Packing List for Northumberland

Northumberland's weather can be unpredictable, so it's best to prepare for all seasons in one day—especially if you plan on exploring the coast, castles, and countryside.

Essentials for All Travelers:

- Waterproof jackets and layers – Sudden rain showers are common, even in summer.
- Comfortable walking shoes or boots – Many attractions require walking on uneven terrain.
- Portable phone charger and power bank – Some remote areas have limited charging spots.
- Sunscreen and sunglasses – Even on cloudy days, UV exposure can be high.

- Reusable water bottle – Many towns have refill stations to help reduce plastic waste.

For Outdoor Adventurers:

- Map and compass – Some hiking trails, especially in Northumberland National Park, have limited phone signals.
- Binoculars – Ideal for birdwatching, especially on the Farne Islands.
- Backpack with snacks – Many countryside walks have few cafés or shops along the way.

For Winter Travelers:

- Thermal clothing and gloves – Temperatures can drop significantly, especially near the coast.
- Non-slip boots – Snow and ice can make pathways slippery.

Safety Tips for Exploring Remote Areas

Northumberland's landscapes are breathtaking, but some areas can be quite remote. Keep these safety tips in mind to ensure a smooth journey.

- **Check the weather forecast** before heading out. Sudden changes in weather can make hiking or coastal walks dangerous.

- **Plan your route in advance** and let someone know your itinerary if you are heading into the wilderness.
- **Carry a physical map** when hiking, as phone signals can be weak in rural areas.
- **Be aware of tide times** if visiting places like Holy Island. The causeway floods twice a day, and getting stranded can be dangerous.
- **Pack enough food and water** when exploring off-the-beaten-path locations, as shops may be miles away.

Best Apps and Websites for Travel Planning

- **Northumberland National Park App** – Offers detailed hiking trails, maps, and visitor information.
- **Met Office Weather App** – Provides accurate weather forecasts for different areas in Northumberland.
- **National Trust & English Heritage Apps** – Useful for checking opening hours, ticket prices, and historical information.
- **Trainline & Go North East** – Helps with public transport schedules and ticket bookings.
- **What3Words** – Useful for navigation and emergency situations in remote areas.

Responsible Tourism: Protecting Northumberland's Natural Beauty

Northumberland's landscapes and wildlife are precious, and it's important to keep them that way for future generations.

- **Stick to marked trails** to avoid damaging fragile ecosystems.
- **Respect wildlife** by keeping a safe distance, especially when visiting seabird colonies or seal habitats.
- **Take all rubbish with you** and avoid single-use plastics.
- **Support local businesses** by choosing independent cafés, shops, and accommodations.

Why Northumberland Will Steal Your Heart

Northumberland is a place of untamed beauty, where history, nature, and culture come together in a way that few destinations can match. Whether you are drawn to the towering castles, the sweeping beaches, or the warm hospitality of its people, this region has a way of leaving a lasting impression.

From the **rugged coastline of Bamburgh Beach** to the **mystical ruins of Dunstanburgh Castle**, every corner of Northumberland tells a story. The **star-filled**

skies above Kielder, the **charm of its market towns**, and the **timeless landscapes of Hadrian's Wall** are experiences that stay with you long after your visit ends.

So, whether this is your first trip to Northumberland or one of many, there is always something new to discover. One thing is certain—you will leave with memories that will call you back again.

BONUS CHAPTER

3-Day & 7-Day Itineraries for Every Type of Traveler

Whether you're visiting Northumberland for a short weekend break or planning a week-long adventure, these curated itineraries will help you experience the best of this beautiful region. Each itinerary includes travel times, must-see attractions, dining recommendations, and accommodation options.

A Weekend Getaway: The Best of Northumberland in 3 Days

This itinerary is perfect for those who want to experience the highlights of Northumberland in just three days.

Day 1: Castles & Coastline

- **Morning:**
    - Start at **Bamburgh Castle** (9:30 AM – 12:00 PM). Explore this iconic fortress with stunning sea views.
    - Walk down to **Bamburgh Beach** for breathtaking coastal scenery.

- **Lunch:**
  - **Potted Lobster, Bamburgh** – Enjoy fresh seafood in a cozy setting.
- **Afternoon:**
  - Visit **Alnwick Castle & Gardens** (1:30 PM – 4:30 PM). Tour the castle, famous for its Harry Potter filming locations, and explore the beautiful gardens.
- **Dinner:**
  - **The Treehouse Restaurant, Alnwick** – A magical dining experience among the treetops.
- **Stay Overnight:**
  - **The Cookie Jar, Alnwick** – A boutique hotel in a former convent, offering luxurious comfort.

Day 2: Holy Island & Coastal Wonders

- **Morning:**
  - Drive to **Holy Island (Lindisfarne)** – Check tide times before crossing the causeway.
  - Visit **Lindisfarne Castle & Priory**, explore the historic ruins, and taste **Lindisfarne Mead**.
- **Lunch:**
  - **Pilgrims Coffee House, Holy Island** – Great for homemade soups and pastries.
- **Afternoon:**

- ○ Visit **Dunstanburgh Castle** – Take a scenic coastal walk from Craster to reach these dramatic ruins.
- **Dinner:**
  - ○ **The Jolly Fisherman, Craster** – Famous for its smoked kippers and seafood dishes.
- **Stay Overnight:**
  - ○ **Doxford Hall Hotel & Spa** – A luxury country house hotel.

Day 3: Countryside & Hadrian's Wall

- **Morning:**
  - ○ Drive to **Hadrian's Wall** and explore **Housesteads Roman Fort**.
- **Lunch:**
  - ○ **Twice Brewed Inn** – A cozy pub with local ales and hearty meals.
- **Afternoon:**
  - ○ Visit **Northumberland National Park** for a short scenic hike.
- **Evening:**
  - ○ Head back or extend your stay with a **stargazing session at Kielder Observatory**.

A Week in Northumberland: A 7-Day Adventure

This itinerary covers all the must-visit attractions at a relaxed pace.

Day 1: Alnwick & Coastal Castles

- **Alnwick Castle & Gardens**
- **Bamburgh Castle**
- Dinner at **The Treehouse Restaurant**

Day 2: Holy Island & Craster

- **Lindisfarne Castle & Priory**
- **Dunstanburgh Castle**
- Craster's **famous kippers** for lunch

Day 3: Hadrian's Wall & Roman Ruins

- **Housesteads Roman Fort**
- **Vindolanda**
- Stargazing at **Kielder Observatory**

Day 4: The Farne Islands

- **Seabird & seal-watching boat tour**
- **Seahouses village exploration**

Day 5: Northumberland National Park & The Cheviots

- Hike **The Cheviot Hills**
- Visit **Rothbury & Cragside House**

Day 6: Berwick-upon-Tweed & Countryside Drives

- Walk the **Elizabethan Walls**
- **River Tweed boat tour**

Day 7: Relaxation & Local Flavors

- Visit **Lindisfarne Mead Distillery**
- Enjoy afternoon tea at **Eshott Hall**

History Buff's Itinerary: Castles & Roman Ruins

This itinerary takes you through Northumberland's most historic sites.

- **Day 1:** Alnwick Castle, Warkworth Castle
- **Day 2:** Bamburgh Castle, Lindisfarne Castle
- **Day 3:** Dunstanburgh Castle, Berwick-upon-Tweed
- **Day 4:** Hadrian's Wall, Housesteads Roman Fort

- **Day 5:** Vindolanda, Chesters Roman Fort
- **Day 6:** Cragside House & Gardens
- **Day 7:** Berwick Barracks & Town Walls

Nature Lover's Itinerary: Hiking, Wildlife & Stargazing

For those who love outdoor adventures.

- **Day 1:** The Cheviot Hills, Harthope Valley
- **Day 2:** Farne Islands boat tour
- **Day 3:** Druridge Bay & Hauxley Wildlife Discovery Centre
- **Day 4:** Hadrian's Wall walk
- **Day 5:** Kielder Water & Forest Park
- **Day 6:** Stargazing at Kielder Observatory
- **Day 7:** Northumberland National Park

Romantic Itinerary for Couples: Coastal Sunsets & Luxury Stays

Perfect for a honeymoon or special getaway.

- **Day 1:** Stay at **Doxford Hall**, enjoy spa treatments

- **Day 2:** Visit **Lindisfarne Castle**, watch the sunset on the beach
- **Day 3:** Private boat tour around **Coquet Island**
- **Day 4:** Horseback riding on **Bamburgh Beach**
- **Day 5:** Enjoy a romantic dinner at **Potted Lobster, Bamburgh**
- **Day 6:** Explore **Cragside House** & gardens
- **Day 7:** Afternoon tea at **Eshott Hall**

Relaxed Itinerary for Seniors: Scenic Drives & Easy Walks

Ideal for a slower-paced holiday with easy accessibility.

- **Day 1:** Visit **Alnwick Castle & Gardens** (mobility-friendly)
- **Day 2:** Take a scenic drive along the **Northumberland Coastal Route**
- **Day 3:** Explore **Holy Island** (accessible routes available)
- **Day 4:** Take a **boat cruise on the River Tweed**
- **Day 5:** Visit **Cragside House**, enjoy a leisurely walk in the gardens
- **Day 6:** Enjoy the **Kielder Water cruise**
- **Day 7:** Relax at a **luxury countryside retreat**

Northumberland's Itineraries

No matter what type of traveler you are, Northumberland has something for everyone. Whether you're here for a short visit or a longer stay, the combination of **history, nature, culture, and hospitality** ensures an unforgettable experience.

Northumberland Travel Guide 2025

MAPS

How To Scan

- Open the Camera App
- Point at the QR Code
- Wait for the Notification
- Tap the Notification
- Follow the Instructions to view map

Northumberland Map

How To Scan

- Open the Camera App
- Point at the QR Code
- Wait for the Notification
- Tap the Notification
- Follow the Instructions to view map

Hadrian's Wall Map

Northumberland Travel Guide 2025

How To Scan

- Open the Camera App
- Point at the QR Code
- Wait for the Notification
- Tap the Notification
- Follow the Instructions to view map

Bamburgh Castle Map

134

How To Scan

- Open the Camera App
- Point at the QR Code
- Wait for the Notification
- Tap the Notification
- Follow the Instructions to view map

Alnwick Castle Map

Northumberland Travel Guide 2025

How To Scan

- Open the Camera App
- Point at the QR Code
- Wait for the Notification
- Tap the Notification
- Follow the Instructions to view map

Warkworth Castle Map

Printed in Great Britain
by Amazon